GIRL

THE SEX THE FUN
THE JEALOUSY THE GOSSIP
THE SUCCESS THE STRUGGLES
THE MARRIAGE THE DIVORCE
THE BEAUTY THE WARMTH
THE WORK THE FAMILY
THE DREAMS THE CAREER
THE HUSBANDS THE KIDS
THE LAUGHTER THE TEARS
THE SECRETS THE SUPPORT
THE LOVERS THE FIGHTERS
THE BALANCE THE INTUITION
THE THIGHS THE SHOES THE DIETS
THE TRUST THE LOYALTY THE LIES
THE INTELLECT THE ELEGANCE
THE CONFIDENCE THE DOUBT
THE MOTHERS THE DAUGHTERS
THE COMPASSION THE COURAGE
THE HUMOR THE PASSION
THE LOVE THE FRIENDSHIP

Get Yourself Together™

robynSPEAKS!

STAY COMMITTED TO YOUR OWN HAPPINESS

Much Success!
R. Y. Smith

ROBYN Y. SMITH

Girl...Get Yourself Together –
Stay Committed to Your Own Happiness
ISBN 978-1-105-67465-5

Success Builders Network & robynSPEAKS
Brandywine, Maryland

Published by LuLu Publishing

Contents

Dedication

First, I would like to dedicate this book and the entire "No More Drama" Movement to that constant voice I hear in my ear, whenever I start to "trip" or overthink or over dramatize everyday life events. Consistently I would hear that voice say to me, Girl…Get Yourself Together, until finally, I decided to do just that!

Then, as always, I thank my husband Jeff, daughters Najma and Simone for allowing me to DO what I teach about…**pursue my dream**!

It's appreciated in ways I may never be able to articulate, but I will always keep trying to show how much it means to me to have you guys in my corner*! The Smith Family ROCKS!*

Introduction

"Your happiness is not a frivolous, expendable luxury. The pursuit of happiness is an inalienable right guaranteed by the Declaration of Independence. But we have to be willing to pursue it. Ultimately, genuine happiness can only be realized once we commit to making it a personal priority in our lives." Sarah Breathnach's

I'll bet there are times you can really imagine making **yourself** and **your happiness** a personal priority – and you may even get excited about that thought for a while…

But then, real life kicks in, and you're back to the same old same old. And not only are you back to the same old same old, you may even be beating yourself up for it because you think you *should* know better by now.

Sound familiar?

If it does, it's because you're not alone. Even in America, less than 15% of individuals report ever achieving the goals they believed they could achieve.

Less than 15%. In other words, they are always wanting and NEVER getting.

Always asking…but not figuring out a way to actually RECEIVE the life they had envisioned for themselves and the happiness they deserve.

But here's the good news.

You AREN'T like the masses. YOU ARE A DIFFERENT KIND OF CHIC!

What I have found is that women who are drawn to books such as ***Girl…Get Yourself Together***, already have ***part*** of what it takes to begin receiving what they want! In other words, they are poised to start receiving and achieving the life they envision. They just need a handful of simple steps and the right kind of support and everything starts to change!

You are Poised to

Receive!

1

Girl…Get Yourself Together! (Getting a Grip on Where You are and Where You Need to Be)

"Where am I and how in the world did I get here?"

Women all across this nation are waking up and asking themselves this question. We live this life, day by day, day in and day out, just going about life as it is handed to us. We never stop to observe this life we have created for ourselves. At some point we start to question: Who chose this? Is this what I truly want? Is this who I truly am?

If you think about it, we aren't taught or encouraged to be authentic. From birth, we were taught and commanded to stay within the lines. From our first breath on earth, those who were tasked with caring for us and taking care of us (doctors, parents, teachers, etc.) began imposing on us their rules, values, procedures and beliefs about how the world works, who we should be and how we should navigate ourselves in this world's system.

Now, trust me, I'm the mom of two awesome daughters and I truly understand the need for guidance, training and how necessary this process is. But it does lead to one of life's greatest dilemmas...how do we truly discover who we are when we learn about life through the filtered perspective of those who raised us and the culture we grew up in? Think about it; what if we were allowed to try things, which perhaps our parents didn't agree with or what if we were allowed to do things, which perhaps our parents had never tried. What would life be like for us, for you, for me and is it too late to find out?

The first step to getting anywhere in life is to first determine where you are and how you got there. Then, set the path that leads to where you want to be.

So, where are you?

Awareness is the first step in the creation process. As you grow in self-awareness, you will better understand why you feel what you feel and why you behave as you behave. That understanding then gives you the opportunity and freedom to change those things you'd like to change about yourself and create the life you want. Without fully knowing who you are, self-acceptance and change become impossible.

Having clarity about who you are and what you want (and why you want it), empowers you to **consciously and actively** make those wants a reality. Otherwise, you'll continue to get "caught up" in your own internal dramas and unknown beliefs, allowing unknown thought processes to determine your feelings and actions.

If you think about it, not understanding why you do what you do, and why you feel what you feel, is like going through your life with a stranger's mind. How do you make wise decisions and choices if you don't understand why you want what you want? It's a difficult and chaotic way to live; never knowing what this stranger is going to do next.

Who's the expert? When we want good, solid information, we turn to the experts. So, who are you going to turn to for information about yourself? Who's the expert?

You Are!

Does a friend, a therapist, a minister, your hero, your spouse, your parents know more about you than you? They can't. You live in your skin and mind 24 hours a day, 7 days a week, 52 weeks a year, day in and day out, no one's closer to you than you! The answers are in there, perhaps all you've needed to solve your riddles is a useful question.

Questions can help you become more self-aware. Are you where you live? Are you your job? Are you what you look like? The answers to these questions are only reflections of who you are to the outside world. But it's just that, a reflection of your inner self. To go below the surface, the questions need to be more meaningful.

What type of people do I enjoy spending time with?
Well...they have to be open-minded people. I really enjoy their company.

Why do I enjoy being with open-minded people?
Because then I can explore lots of different ideas. I enjoy searching for answers. And if they're open-minded, the exploration can go anywhere!

What do I mean by "exploration can go anywhere"?
I mean I can investigate all the big questions in life like...Why are we here or where do emotions come from?

How does being with open-minded people assist me in exploring those questions?
Well...if they're open-minded they won't make fun of my ideas.

Do you see where this is going? Great! The more you commit to discovering the real YOU the more likely you will actually become who you were meant to be!

2

Stop Trying to FIT IN: The Quest for Authenticity!

William Shakespeare said, *"God has given you one face, and you make yourself another."* The overwhelming influence of our upbringing, our surroundings and our experiences, certainly play a major role in who we have become. However, our response to life's circumstances and how we internalize what we experience, has everything to do with who we are and "how" we are, and more to the point, how we engage with others and ourselves. In other words, it's really, not so much what happens to us that has presented the challenge, but how we responded to them. It's how we allowed these external forces to shape our lives and ultimately create this inauthentic person that we have now become.

When the world dictates how you should live your life, it can actually become harder to be true to your *authentic* self.

Success will always find you when you are authentic. Follow your happiness and you will always feel joy, and when you feel joy, success finds you.

Why do so many of us wear masks and hide who we really are? Everyone is born authentic, but as we grow up, we spend so much time separating from who we are, acting as if we were something different, and creating that "other face". Acting is stressful, especially, when you are as bad at it as I am! Being true to who we are takes time and effort, but it is so much less stressful than going through life being someone we were never meant to be.

To be authentic means to find the key to happiness and success within one's self, *not within society*.

When you live an authentic life, you are living the life that resonates with your soul! As the saying goes, "We are not human beings having a spiritual experience. We are spiritual beings having a human experience."

It takes courage, honesty and desire to be free of other's opinions. To quote my favorite saying, *"What you think of me is none of my business."*

To be authentic, you have to stop putting other's needs ahead of your own, and you have to stop compromising your dreams to please others.

Side Note: Don't be so judgmental and opinionated with your friends either! Allow them the freedom to choose their own life's plan as well.

Now, this is all great and dandy, but how do we get down to the core of who we really are and stay true to ourselves?

Here are a few questions to ask:

What in life already makes you happy?

Sometimes we get so busy and consumed with what's **not** right in our lives, we fail to take an inventory of the things we currently have or experience that actually make us happy! I suppose the "bad" sometimes screams louder than the good and therefore becomes our focus. However, we have to make a conscience effort to focus on those things that add to our quality of life; those things that make us feel good and then, more importantly, figure out why those things put smiles on our faces.

The power to define is the power to become! If you take a true introspect of what makes you happy, you may find that you can re-create your "happy place" at will!

What, if added to your life, would make you happier?

What's missing? This missing part keeps you from being happy and completely satisfied with your life. You keep searching for the right thing but you can't find it. You then get frustrated about your life and nothing brings pleasure anymore.

Look around your life. Are you really missing something or is it just an illusion? Do you set misguided goals for yourself? Goals based on what's 'supposed' to make you happy rather than on what really will?

If you think that you are not as happy as you want to be, please remember, that even the happiest people in the world have bad spells in their lives, they just know how to deal with them. If you think that you are not rich enough, you need to know that you will never be truly rich, if money is the only thing you are chasing after. Even if you have millions, it won't be enough.

You already have everything you need and everything you need is within you. Stop saying "I will be happy only when/if … " BE HAPPY and live your life right now. Be the person you are and stop chasing the phantoms of your past or your future.

Do you have the courage to live more authentically?

Being bold is one of the most essential and sometimes the most difficult aspects of authenticity. Living our lives in a bold and authentic way takes real guts and commitment. This doesn't mean that you won't get scared, we all do, it just means that we are willing to act in the face of those fears and are able and willing to stay true to ourselves and what's important to us, even when it gets difficult.

Having courage, as it relates to being yourself and living with authenticity, has to do with getting in touch with your deepest truths, passions and desires in life and then being big and bad enough to make up your mind to live that life "out loud"!

I remember when I was challenged to simply be me! To discover what I loved and to commit to making what I did, reflect who I truly was. I admit it was a challenge; growing up, there were certain labels and expectations placed on me very early on. I was the responsible one, the one who would be successful – you know the type! But what wasn't amplified and developed in me, was the primary reason people believed in my imminent success in the first place... my independence, my creativity, my determination to get things done and in a big way. No one ever encouraged me to use that energy toward things that were important to ME. Instead, I worked hard for everyone else! I became the "go-to" girl; the one who could make it happen for anyone and at any time!

I loved it! It's actually why I love helping people today! But at some point, I lost myself. I could take **your** ideas and make **your** dreams come true without ever giving any thought to what **my** dreams were and whether they were coming true.

The day finally came, when I looked around at all I had achieved, all the success I had experienced from my business ventures and all the success I was witnessing in the lives of my girls, my husband and those I had assisted over the years and I thought to myself…Why am I unhappy? Suddenly, the big house on the hill, the fancy cars in the driveway and the shoes and bags in the closet (Well, wait…the shoes and the bags still bring me great joy!) weren't enough. Nothing reflected who I really was. It was then that I decided, regardless of what anyone else thought, I was going to introduce the world to ME! The real me and all the quirkiness that went along with it!

It caused some feathers to be ruffled at first. I wasn't always there to take care of "them"...NO! I had things that I needed to take care of for ME! It caused me to face some harsh realities as well. The fact that I created these monsters in my life and now had to handle them with kid gloves as I ushered them into my new reality! It took guts and determination, but I did it! And so will you!

How did I make the jump to living an authentic life?

I stepped out! I began asking myself "the question" everyday! What is the question? ***"If today were my last day on this earth, what would I do? What would I say?"*** Yeah, it's a little melodramatic, I know, but we waste our days doing so many insignificant things and yet leave the things that really bring us joy for later. A healthy awareness of what's really important, on a daily basis, can alter the way we live our lives and the way we approach the different scenarios of our days.

I began to dream again! I started thinking about the dreams I had and the goals I had yet to pursue. I discovered that the more I began to get in touch with some of my deepest goals and dreams; I simultaneously began to feel alive, viable and happy! We were all uniquely created with a purpose and, I believe, specific life assignments. We are not here to simply exist; we are here to make a difference;

to make a mark on this world that cannot be erased, as Dr. Creflo Dollar would say.

You have to be careful not to fall into the "merely existing status". Life is more than that. Many people, especially women, seem to simply exist rather than live. Existing is cold and lifeless; people who simply exist are more machine than human. They have their lives running on a sort of autopilot, but they don't seem to know it.

People who just exist usually follow the same routine day in and day out. They wake up, upset that they have to go to work, head out the door, get angry at the same bad drivers or the same bad traffic, run into the same type of problems with the same people or clients at work, come home in the same mood, go through the same means of entertainment, have the same type of arguments with their family members... wash, rinse, repeat.

These people aren't necessarily unhappy, they may be fairly content with their little routine, but they are stuck in a sort of rut, in a bubble, they run the same patterns over and over.

They tend not to learn from their mistakes, perhaps they learn from specific mistakes in specific situations, but they never learn from the thinking that caused the mistakes in the first place.

They are also victims of their emotions, when someone cuts them off, they get angry, when someone starts an argument with them, they get defensive, when something happens in their lives, they react to it without control as to how they react.

They believe they are stuck in their life situation and blame the world and the government and the system for their troubles. Perhaps they call it bad luck. They believe their own happiness depends on the outside world rather than it depending on themselves.

Some of these people love to mindlessly follow rules, even if the intention behind the rules doesn't apply to the situation. They are the type of people who only do things based on society's view of how acceptable it is. They fear stepping out of the bounds of what's normal or accepted. They worry about the opinions of others and try their best to fit in at the expense of their own authenticity. They can't be real.

They generally don't have real dreams, goals or aspirations, and even if they say they do, they take no action to achieve them, or they write them off as something to be done in the future, or perhaps something impossible for them to ever do.

They like mindless entertainment and distractions, anything to keep them from seeing how their lives are passing them by, anything to suppress their desire for something more.

They tend to be more close minded, they have a sort of tunnel vision and only like things that are normal. They resist that which is different.

New ideas and concepts are seen as a waste of time or even threatening to how they see the world.

They are the type of people who hold on to the ideas shared by society, even if the ideas are shown to be untrue.

They are the type that would persecute the great minds of the past for their unique viewpoints and insights, the type who would have argued that the world was flat.

We see this in people all around us and if we are completely honest with ourselves, we see this in ourselves, or have seen it at some point or another.

When I saw myself slipping into the state of merely existing and fitting in, I was determined to dream again and LIVE!

I chose to live a proactive life rather than a reactive one. You have the ability to choose how you respond to situations. Don't allow your environment or the people in it to control how you feel or how you dream.

Take responsibility for your life, for your successes and your failures. Recognize that you have the ability to change your life situation if you aren't happy with it. Seek out new ways to solve your problems; begin to ask constructive questions such as "How can I handle this better?"

You deserve an amazing life. Don't limit yourself by accepting mediocrity. Strive to be happier and to grow over time. Set yourself to accomplish more!

Try to remove negativity from your life. Spend your time dreaming, planning and doing things that make you feel good.

Make the commitment! Have an authentic moment every day. Whether it is telling your friend what she can do with her opinion of you and all of her unsolicited advice, or directing your mother to find someone else's life to meddle in! Do whatever it takes to take this stance and to finally get yourself together!

You truly have to know who you are and begin loving YOU in order to take this bold stance! No worries, we will discuss this more in Chapter 3! This time around, you are actually going to make it happen for yourself

Take a stand each day, and you'll be happier, healthier and attracting the life that you really desire.

3

Discovering the Real YOU!

Do you really know YOU? Have you noticed how fast we can usually see what is missing in the lives of the people around us? What would you say about yourself, if you didn't know yourself? Would you see a workaholic who spends every free minute working on a new project but forgets about her husband and children? Would you see a housewife whose life is limited to the house and taking care of her family? Would you see a person who desperately needs to take care of her health? Do not be partial to yourself, be honest.

One of the toughest things I have ever had to do was to debug this person I had become and truly discover who I really was. Trying to figure out who you are seems relatively straightforward. After all, no one spends more time around you than you. But answering the question of how well you know yourself is actually really tricky. Getting to know yourself means understanding your behavior and responses to certain situations. What will I discover? Will I like what I see?

Fortunately, there are some great ways to get to know yourself better.

Spend some time with YOU!

One of the better ways to really get to know who you are is to spend time alone with your thoughts. Despite what this sounds like, it doesn't mean just sitting in a chair thinking. You can do a lot of things as long as they don't involve brain-numbing activities such as TV.

I personally practice meditation, but you can also workout at the gym, run, read or even do yard work. Anything that gets you in a relaxed, but active state of mind, will work well. This is the ideal state to learn about yourself.

Once you're in this state of mind, you will start noticing and questioning your behaviors and actions. Focus on something you've done that you can't fully explain the reasoning behind. These are the areas of yourself you don't understand. I think everyone has done something, at least once in their lives, that they didn't truly understand why. It can take some time, but you'll find it.

Try to view yourself as objectively as possible. See yourself, not through your own eyes, but as if you are a different person. I did this recently and made a huge revelation about myself.

For many years, I've had friends who've told me I was bossy. However, I refused to believe them! In my mind, being bossy was a negative trait and since I'm not a negative person, I couldn't be like that. Eventually, I looked at myself objectively and realized that, yes, I am bossy! But what is perceived as bossiness is just my way of loving, protecting and teaching. Before that realization, I had been unaware of a facet of who I was and thus, adjustments could never have been made. I'm still a little bossy, LOL, but my awareness of this fact changes my approach to situations and people, which I am sure is a welcomed improvement!

You Are Always Changing

As a human being, you're constantly going through character changes. I'll try to explain this without getting too philosophical about it. Imagine all the things you did and liked when you were five years old. More than likely there is a long list of differences between who you were then and who you are now.

For example, when I was younger, I hated vegetables and now I am a vegetarian! When I was younger, I watched a lot of television and now I hardly turn the television on.

Can I really say that I'm the same person as when I was younger? NO.

Personalities change through time. Keep this in mind when you look at yourself and when you deal with others. Your understanding of who you are now could be based on an older version of yourself. It might be time to update that understanding.

Another thing to remember is that you're going to be continually changing for the rest of your life. It's important to always be aware of who you are and who you are becoming. Who knows, maybe I'll come full circle later on in my own life and start hating vegetables and loving television again…God forbid!!!

You're much deeper and complex than you probably realize. Human emotions and behaviors can't always be explained away in a few sentences.

Understanding yourself is a never-ending process. And ultimately, it takes a lifetime. But you are taking the journey and accepting the challenge, which is much more than what others are willing to do or even contemplating doing. You are a woman who is going to be able to proclaim, my latter days are far greater than my former days, all because you recognize, that through all that you have accomplished in your life, you were a mess! We all were, but now we are awesome, amazing and getting it all together!

4

Be F.L.Y. (First Love Yourself) Making YOU and Your Happiness THE Priority!

Did you notice I said "THE" priority and not "A" priority? "A" priority still gives other things and people the right to get a place in the priority line ahead of you. You must condition yourself to become "THE" priority in your life.

One piece of advice that I give to all of my clients is that we should act in our own best interests. When first introduced to this concept, my initial reaction was to feel uncomfortable – like most people, I worry that I'm being selfish if I put myself first.

When I was a child I was never taught about self-care or to want things. Whenever I wanted something, I was accused of being selfish. It didn't matter if I was tired or just not wanting to do chores. I heard it so much and so often and didn't want to think I was anything bad like that, I stopped taking care of myself in many different ways. If taking care of me was *selfish*, than taking care of and pleasing others was *unselfish.* And I'd much rather be unselfish.

I suspect many people and maybe more women are taught this self-defeating, unloving attitude by other women – mostly their mothers who had learned the same thing in their early lives.

If you experienced something like that somewhere in your past, you might find it difficult to rest enough, difficult to eat well, difficult to take care of your body in other ways. You might find it difficult to take care of yourself in relationships. You might judge your emotions as unworthy of a good 'unselfish' person. You might also find it difficult to have healthy boundaries and difficult to stand up for what you know is right.

But I've come to realize that acting in your own best interests, when done properly, isn't a selfish act – it's a way to ensure that you're making the very best of your life, so that you can help those around you to make the very best of theirs.

The struggle for most women is understanding the difference between *selfish* and *self-care* and then, once they understand the difference, how to put their understanding of *self-care* into practice.

There is a major difference between selfish and self-care.

Selfish: Acting in your own self-interest – without regard for others.

Self-Care: Acting in your own self-interest – so that you can be your best for yourself and for others.

When people are behaving selfishly, they are foolishly taking care of themselves **at the cost of others**. In fact, behaving selfishly does NOT end up taking care of anyone because if we do things at the cost of others, or without regard for others, we are literally shooting ourselves in the foot.

I'm sure you can take a look around you and notice where we all have behaved selfishly. Now look within yourself. When you behave selfishly, don't you feel like you just got away with something? Most of you are very conscientious women, so I know you know what I'm talking about.

But self-CARE is different. The word "care" as a noun means "serious attention" and as a verb "to have thought or regard". Now we add "self" to the definition and we come up with "serious attention to the self" and "to have thought or regard for the self". It doesn't say ANYTHING about "regardless of others"!

So let's get very clear here, when you are about to do something, be it reading a book, a massage or sign up for a course, ask yourself if you are doing this "regardless of others". Have integrity with yourself – are you busting your budget? Are you hurting another person with your actions or are you simply investing in yourself? Only you know the answer. I recommend that you be truthful with yourself so that you will be dealing in reality, not in illusion.

I have seen women get these two concepts twisted. They go from always caring for others to ONLY caring about themselves! You can get your "ME" time without ignoring your family. Self-care and making YOU the priority means being committed to setting aside "ME" time and being responsible enough to make sure the other areas of your life accommodates this requirement.

I set aside 2 hours every morning (5:00am – 7:00am) for my morning reflections. No one gets any attention during this time but ME! But at the same time, I made sure that my family had no needs during that time, therefore, it doesn't take from them – it only adds to me!

I also set aside every Friday! Yep, no working, no errands for the family, nothing but me, me, me! But, my family agreed to this time! They have no expectations for any attention until I arrive back home!

Here's how I know my ME time isn't selfish…it seems everyone else always benefit from it! I come home with gifts, or in a great mood, or with great ideas for family time! That's what putting ME first does; it allows me freedom of thought and expression.

The other stumbling block here for most of you is GUILT. I see, so often in my coaching sessions, how many of you are led by guilt. Somewhere along the line you have been taught that taking care of yourself is a "guilty pleasure". That is the mindset of the survivor and the victim.

When you make YOU the priority you get clear and focused on your goals. You have energy to bring about your dreams and visions. You are receptive to opportunities that support your dreams and goals. You are receptive to what your body needs. You receive love and you get to know what EASE actually means!

You deserve to have a successful, empowering and powerful life.

Invest in YOU!

Take a moment and look at yourself in the mirror. No, not a mirror in the physical sense, but look at yourself from the outside. How do you look to others? How valuable are you to those around you? Do you stand out as an important asset, or do you slip by as just a run-of-the-mill person? These are difficult questions to answer, and the answers may not always be obvious.

Becoming a valuable asset is important on both the professional and personal level. When most people talk about investing in themselves, it has to do with getting ahead in the workplace. This is certainly important if you're trying to keep your job, advance your career, or enter a new line of work, but it is equally important on a personal level. These two aspects of your life are more interconnected than you may imagine. Investing in your professional life will impact aspects of your personal life, and investing in yourself on a personal level will undoubtedly help your professional life.

Invest in Your Health

Before you can make improvements in other areas of your life you must first take care of some of your most basic needs. We need to step back for a moment and forget about money. Money is important, but without your health, it's worthless. Understandably, you're probably groaning at the idea of what it will take to improve your health. You're thinking about diets, lots of exercise, and cutting out all the fun stuff in your life. I agree, none of that sounds like much fun. But we're not talking about making drastic changes overnight. Habits that have developed over the course of years can be hard to break, so it's best to make small changes over time that will lead to healthier habits.

1. Get More Sleep

We live in a 24 hour world and it is taking its toll on sleep. Between the internet, TV, Blackberries and iPhones, the day doesn't end when you come home from work. These days, we're constantly being interrupted and our work lives are bleeding into our personal lives. This added stress and lack of down time can really cut into your sleep. While it isn't uncommon for people to get by on just six hours or so of sleep, studies have shown most of us still need more.

I know, I know. There are only 24 hours in a day and you already can't get everything done, so how on Earth can you be expected to get more sleep? If you like to hit the snooze button 5 times every morning, find you can't concentrate until you've had your first three cups of coffee in the morning, or could pass out at your desk after lunch, then you're not getting enough sleep. Think about all of the time you waste when you aren't completely focused or working inefficiently because you're fighting the urge to sleep.

Instead, use that extra hour you're wasting throughout the day by being tired and get some extra sleep. You'll wake up feeling better, your body will be rested, and you can make better use of your waking hours, not to mention improve your overall health.

2. Eat Better

This doesn't mean you should go on a drastic diet and try to cut 20 pounds in a month, but just a few little changes in your diet can go a long way. Start with breakfast. It really is the most important meal of the day. Breakfast will jump-start your metabolism and prepare your body for a full day of work. I always had difficulty finding time in the morning to squeeze in breakfast, but I've found that just grabbing a banana or a piece of veggie bacon before starting my day helps a lot.

Next, just be a little more conscious of what you're eating and make an effort to make small changes here and there. If you drink a few sodas each day, start by replacing one with something else to drink. Ideally water, but even juice or something would be a good start. Over time you'll find that you crave soda less and in the process be cutting out a lot of calories from your diet. If you're looking to cut back come dinner time, consider cutting back on some of the pasta or rice and throw in an occasional salad. Again, even if you do this just a couple times a week you will begin to create healthy habits that will lead to a healthier you over time.

3. Go to the Doctor

Medicine has come a long way in recent years, but nothing beats preventative medicine. Why wait until you have symptoms before going to the doctor? By then it might be too late and your only option might be something drastic. Unfortunately, the cost of health care is a major problem in this country so it's no wonder so many people put off going to the doctor until absolutely necessary. **But if you have health insurance, use it and if you don't, get some or check with your state Health Department for subsidized medical assistance.** ***(Yes, I believe in using all benefits due to me when my financial situation warrants it.)***

There's no doubt about it, going to the doctor is an inconvenience if you aren't sick. You may have to go late after work, take a few hours off, and otherwise waste a good part of your day. At the minimum, you should be at least getting your annual check-up. It might not be the most exciting appointment in your calendar book, but if you can help keep tabs on your health and possibly receive advanced warning of a serious problem that may develop in the future, the last thing on your mind will be the few hours you "wasted" by going to the doctor.

4. Invest in Your Personal Self

What's important to you? That's what we're going to try and answer right now. Take a moment to think about what you really enjoy and what matters most to you. Spending time with friends? Family? Being outdoors? Helping others? Just reading a good book? Now that you have an answer, how often do you get to do these things? If you're like most people, the answer is probably, "not often enough." Life is too short to be stuck running around constantly trying to meet deadlines, make more money, and constantly putting things off until the future. You need to make time for the things you love.

6. Invest in Your Professional Self

A healthier and happier you can go a long way, but if you really want to invest in something that can pay huge dividends, consider investing in your professional self. It doesn't matter if you're making minimum wage doing factory work or a veteran executive with a corner office — investing in yourself will shape your future.

Take a class, start meaningful networking, join associations; whatever needs to be done in order to improve your professional position in life, make a commitment to invest in your professional goals and dreams.

5

Manage the Business of YOU

Have you ever taken a real good introspection of where you are in certain areas of your life and said, "You know what…I am so much BETTER than this?"

Well, here's the newsflash: No one is perfect! You could be a superstar in so many areas of your life, yet a colossal mess in another! Well, first things first...a few messed up areas, mismanaged moments and bad decisions don't define who you are. Only you can do that.

But more importantly, when you gain these perspectives, you need to be big enough to manage those areas of your life. If you are better, then act like it and get yourself together!

Stop Trying to Be Superwoman!

Superwoman Syndrome is exactly what it says it is - trying to be Superwoman. You are a woman who feels pressured to be able to do it all. You are a woman who works hard to fill multiple roles. You are a woman who is trying to juggle, family, career and social activities.

And more often than not, if you have Superwoman Syndrome, you are feeling overworked, overwhelmed and overly committed. You are also probably exhausted, anxious and stressed to the max. But don't worry - you are not alone.

Those who have Superwoman Syndrome are moms, professionals, community organizers, activists, volunteers and socialites. Young girls and college-aged women are also susceptible if they are under pressure to excel in school, sports, looks and relationships. Some reports show that girls as young as 13 suffer from Superwoman Syndrome. WOW!

You can't do it all, and even if you could, that doesn't mean you should! Give yourself a break or you'll burn yourself out.

In the last 30 years or so, since the sexual revolution and the dawn of the equal rights movement, women's roles have been undergoing a drastic change.

More and more women have broken through the glass ceiling, taking ever increasing roles in the corporate world while still juggling family and personal responsibilities. The notion of being superwoman has taken hold and it is a cycle many women can't seem to break.

Technology has made it easier to take on too much

As our lives have become more inundated by technology, the ability to juggle multiple responsibilities at once has been streamlined. Now a woman can hold her entire schedule in one hand, flipping through her virtual rolodex, setting up appointments, solving household problems, all on the fly. But just because it is easier to do, doesn't mean you should be doing it.

Trying to be all things to all people takes a considerable toll on you, both physically and emotionally. Simply put, the more you try to do, the less of yourself you are actually able to give, because your energy reserves just can't handle it.

Stress can cause your body to break down, and with it, your emotions can spiral out of control.

The effects of stress are not just mental

Doctors have proven the effect stress can have on the human body. Everything from disrupting your sleep schedule to short-circuiting your nervous system to increasing fatigue can result from having an overload of stress in your daily life. Your body can only take so much and when your body shuts down, your mind does too.

Oh no…here comes the temper tantrums! Bursts of anger, fits of crying, feelings of anxiety can all begin to creep up until you feel like you just can't handle what life is throwing at you anymore. It's a vicious circle and only you have to power to step up and make it stop.

Take control and become the manager of YOU!

There is no need to feel like you have to do it all. Instead, take a step back, breathe deeply and consider what you really need to do. Keep your priorities straight and try to focus on what is really important. That may mean having to let a few things slide and if that enables you to function better, then isn't it worth it?

We all like to think that we're invincible, but the truth is we're not. We're human and that means we occasionally need to stop and recharge our batteries.

Those electronic devices that run our lives may not slow down, but that doesn't mean we shouldn't. Unplug for a few hours every day and reconnect with the people in your life who really matter. That will mean much more than getting one more item checked off your to-do list.

Yes, women are strong and capable and can handle anything life throws at them, but that doesn't mean we have to handle it all at once. Stop trying to be superwoman and settle for just being **a super woman**, one who's in touch with herself and taking care of her basic needs, then everyone in your life will reap the rewards!

6

Discover your WHY

Do you ever feel like you've accomplished a lot but still feel as is something is missing?

You may know what you are passionate about but not sure what direction to take. Or you may have thought you were following your dream but now feel disconnected from what you are doing and don't know why.

You crave the ability to go through each day with greater satisfaction and enjoyment.

To the outside world, everything looks good but you can't stop feeling empty on the inside knowing there's something more to life that you can't quite put your finger on. Don't feel bad, you're not alone!

So many of us have beaten ourselves up; trying to figure out our purpose and striving for greater meaning in our lives. I have personally struggled with this challenge for most of my career, looking to others for guidance and direction, spending countless hours reading books and blogs and attending seminars to help me find my way.

Is success in life measured only in terms of the money you earn or by the position you reach in your career?

According to me, what matters more than money or the position you hold, is the quality of life you are living. You might be successful and have all the money in the world, but if your quality of life is poor, then you may not be living a happy life. Simply put, success alone will not bring happiness to life.

Quality of life does not necessarily depend on monetary success. A content and happy life needs more than money. A passionate life is much more than achieving success.

So, are we living the life which realizes our true potential? Are we living a happy life? Are we living a passionate life?

The Power of WHY

What's *your* Why? What compels you to get up and go to work each day, to do things you don't want to, and to put up with your boss? Everyone needs some motivation to keep on track, and it has to be a strong image. What is yours?

If you can't close your eyes and see your *Why* in detail, now is a good time to get clarity. Ask yourself the following questions:

- When were you at your happiest?
- What were you doing?
- When you close your eyes and picture yourself incredibly happy, what do you see?
- What makes you forget yourself for hours on end?
- When do you feel best about yourself and your surroundings?
- What do you talk about excitedly?

Desires can be subtle. Maybe you have fond memories of staying somewhere. But it might actually be the time with friends that made the place special. What aspect really touches you?

Find some quiet time to get clear on what moves you, and then visualize it until you can see this compelling future as clearly as if it were right before your eyes. You'll know this is working when you look at something you thought you needed and instead see your *Why*.

The Next Step

This is a demanding, complicated world. It takes a lot of work to become good at something, or to get something you really want. Dave Ramsey says, "Live like no one else, so later you can live like no one else!" *Why* work hard when you could just watch TV? *Why* save for some undetermined future when you could watch it on a bigger TV?

Most successful people have spent thousands of hours perfecting what they do. They have a vision of the future and their place in it. Otherwise they wouldn't have bothered with all the work it took to get there. Yet most successful people would tell you that they loved the process — the challenge, the passion, the fun! They've found a vision of the future that compels and excites them, and that's the difference. That's why they are where they are.

In fact, that's why we *all* are where we are — our previous beliefs and vision of the future. Do what you've always done, and you'll have what you've always had. Create a vision that moves you to do things you've never done before, and you'll find yourself in new, wonderful places. **Once you have a Why, no matter how unlikely, the How becomes a lot easier and more enjoyable.**

What's your Why? What do you visualize in the morning to get yourself going? What motivates you to do everything you do?

Sometimes we do things simply because it's what everyone else does or because it's the way things have always been done. Not realizing that perhaps there was a clearly defined WHY for what was done back in the day or for what others are doing, but for you, your WHY became blurry. It's "just the way I do things."

I heard a story about the End of the Ham that illustrates this so well:

A young woman was preparing a ham dinner. After she cut off the end of the ham, she placed it in a pan for baking.

Her friend asked her, "Why did you cut off the end of the ham"?

And she replied,"I really don't know but my mother always did, so I thought you were supposed to."

Later, when talking to her mother, she asked her why she cut off the end of the ham before baking it and her mother replied, "I really don't know, but that's the way

my mom always did it."

A few weeks later while visiting her grandmother, the young woman asked, "Grandma, why is it that you cut off the end of a ham before you bake it?"

Her grandmother replied, "Well dear, otherwise it would never fit into my baking pan."

I love that story because it truly demonstrates how we sometimes fall into a monotony of day in and day out behaviors that are not truly motivated by what means the most to us. Identifying WHY we do what we do is vital in living a purposeful, fulfilled and happy life.

Make your W.H.Y. the flagpole of your decision making. When deciding to do anything that may impact your life ask yourself.

Does it **W**orks toward your goals?
Is this a **H**ealthy decision for myself and my family?
Only say **Y**es, only if the above are in agreement!

7

Develop Mental Toughness

What is the difference between someone who is a champion and someone who is the runner-up? What makes someone able to look an impossible situation in the face and willingly conquer it? It's the same thing that Super Bowl MVP's, successful CEO's, and leaders of all types possess. It is something that you should possess! It may be the one factor that determines whether your goals are realized or not.

In all of my years in school, I don't think that there was any course that specifically taught me how to be mentally tough. Those who play competitive sports may understand mental toughness more than those who do not play sports but just because you played a sport, does not make you mentally tough.

I've been looking for the perfect definition for mental toughness but there seems to be a slight discrepancy on what it actually means. I found a few decent definitions but most of them dealt exclusively with athletics. But since I am convinced that mental toughness is necessary in order to overachieve in many other parts of your life, this is the way I'd like you to understand what mental toughness is.

Mental Toughness- Having a physiological edge that enables you to be consistent, confident, focused, and determined during high pressure situations, in order to perform at maximum potential.

Listen to me ladies, if we are going to do this thing called life and do it right, we need this! People might think that this is a skill or trait that someone is born with. I don't believe that entirely. I'm leaning more towards the idea that some learn how to be mentally tough earlier than others but I stand by the notion that this skill can be learned. It is not an easy attribute to acquire however, that's why so many people don't have it, but trust me, it is well worth the work. Just imagine the advantages of being tough minded!

Being able to bounce back quickly after a setback; Being unshakable through most any circumstance; Able to leap tall buildings in a single bound! Just kidding, but developing mental toughness can be a game changer for you.

Those who are strong minded are not hard to spot. True mental toughness, however is sometimes hard to find. There are many characteristics that a person may possess that may mimic the characteristics of a mentally strong person. If someone is stubborn, opinionated, outspoken, bossy, or demanding, some might see them as being strong minded, But that's not mental toughness. Mental toughness is not usually seen in the actions of a person, rather in the reaction of that person.

You might know a person who seems to be a rock mentally. This person seems to know what they want and know how to get it. Not only that, they have an answer to every question, an opinion for every topic, and an idea for every circumstance. That may seem to be the formula for success in the mind, but what happens when something goes wrong? Or a plan or project fails over and over and over again? This is where those who are mentally tough strive and excel.

There are six major characteristics of mental toughness

Confidence, Focus, Motivation, Courage, Composure and Resiliency

Confidence

Having belief in yourself may increase your mental toughness, if applied correctly. If you believe in your ability to succeed, then you are preparing yourself for success and bracing yourself in case of obstacles.

Focus

When a person cannot stay focused it is easy for them to mentally collapse in high pressure situations. The ability to concentrate on the task at hand and stay focused on that task is an unbelievably important skill that many cannot seem to master.

Motivation

Have you ever been really excited about a goal and then weeks later lose your excitement? Of course you have, everyone has. Finding motivation is easy, keeping motivation is a challenge. Motivation ties in closely with focus because the majority of lost motivation stems from the lack of or a shift in focus. In situations when the climb is uphill, motivation, focus, and resiliency should be your best friends.

Courage

Remember that being courageous is not being fearless; rather it is having fear but acting as if you don't. Acts of courage are usually accompanied by a mountain of fear but a courageous person will do what they have to do in order to get done that which has to get done.

Composure

Roget's New Millennium Dictionary Thesaurus has a lot of good synonyms for composure such as self-possession, coolness, equanimity and control. They have fortitude listed but I think that has more to do with strength and endurance than it does composure.

Resiliency

It doesn't matter how confident, focused, motivated, courageous, or composed you are, if you do not see your goal to the end then it may turn out to be pointless. Being resilient is pushing through until you reach your destination.

Now you should be ready to develop mental toughness and also reap the benefits of having it. I strongly believe that the mind is the most complex and advanced computer the world will ever see. It does what it is programmed to do. What your brain is now is what you have already programmed it to be. You must be aware of how you will react in situation where your mental strength may be tested. In sports, it's knowing how to react when your opponent is stronger, smarter, and faster, than you are. In business, it's knowing what to do when your employees come up short of your expectations, your deadlines are not going to get met, and profits are way down. In your personal life, it's knowing how to deal with heartbreak, handle those who try to con or take advantage of you, and assert yourself in order to project the image of the person you want to be.

This starts with programming the mind to do what you want it to do in those situations. Begin to understand the best possible action or reaction for a circumstance that will require you being mentally tough. I suggest writing down how you would usually react in those situations, then writing down how you would like to react in those situations. See the difference? The shortest distance from point A to point B is a straight line. Start focusing on point B, which is how you want to react, until you begin to feel like you can actually react that way. Run the scenarios in your mind and you will begin to feel more comfortable in your new mind.

Small Steps

Before you can run you need to crawl. Every opportunity that you miss to strengthen your mindset is a step backwards. Be on the lookout for ways that you are acting mentally weak throughout your day. Chances are, your actions and reactions are habits that must be broken. Put in place a small goal or challenge for yourself in order to test your toughness. It is very important that you set groundbreaking yet viable challenges or else the exercise is useless. Do this on a daily basis and you'll begin to notice that the test will begin to become bigger and more challenging. This is because those small steps are becoming larger steps and your mental toughness is growing. Don't stop, keep testing and challenging yourself.

Practice Composure

I hate being nervous. Nervousness is one of the more uncomfortable feelings a person can experience. The tougher you are mentally, the less nervous you will become. People who are constantly nervous are allowing outside circumstances to determine their mood and the outcome of their situation. Now think about it, once you have composure and are in control of yourself, you can then move on to controlling your situation. I can't stress enough how important of a skill this is to learn and master. In fact, I think I'll do some research on it and write about it in my next book. For now, the best way I've found to stay calm and to keep your composure, is to practice calming yourself and preparing yourself for high stress situations. See yourself in these types of situations before they actually occur. Make sure you do this exercise as if it were a real life situation so that you are more equipped to handle the real thing.

Bounce Back Quickly

Obstacles can be discouraging and can create the feeling of failure. Once that feeling is there you may entertain thoughts of giving up the journey. In order for you to bounce back quickly you must prepare yourself for these obstacles internally and externally. Do all that you can to prevent these setbacks from happening, but if they do happen, remind yourself of your goal. Surround yourself with positive people who will encourage you when you are tempted to give up. Keep motivational materials around also. Posting motivational quotes or reading success stories may give you that recharge that you need to keep you going. The quicker you bounce back, the quicker you will reach your goal.

Take initiative, Take Control

If you've dealt with the nervousness issue this shouldn't be that hard. If you've practiced composure, then your mind should be clearer and you should be able to think straight. The clearer your thoughts, the better your decision making will be. At first you may be hesitant to take control if you are not accustomed to doing so. But building toughness is like building muscle, you have to work at it in order to make it stronger.

Look out for opportunities to take control of a situation. Look out for opportunities to do something that requires you to be in control even if it's something that you've never done before. If you are already mentally tough, raise the bar and set a long term challenge that will test the stamina of your toughness.

At the end of Michael Jordan's career there was almost no question that he was the best player in NBA history. Wilt Chamberlain who played in the '60s and '70s had a marvelous career and scored more points in his career than

Jordan did. Wilt even scored 100 points in a game. But when it was all said and done, Jordan was still seen as the greatest. Why? As one analyst pointed out Jordan had an amazing ability to excel his performance in a clutch situation. Mentally, he intimidated his opponents, and was never intimidated by his opponents. His tough mindedness made the difference in his life and it can make the difference in yours.

If you are going to commit to your happiness and successfully and freely navigate through your complex and dynamic life, developing mental toughness is going to be your number one asset!

Let's do this ladies!

8

Discover Your Purpose!

How do you discover your real purpose in life? I'm not talking about your job, your daily responsibilities, or even your long-term goals. I mean the real reason why you're here at all — the very reason you exist.

Perhaps you're that person who doesn't believe you have a purpose and that life has no meaning. It doesn't matter; not believing that you have a purpose won't prevent you from discovering it, just as a lack of belief in gravity won't prevent you from tripping. All that a lack of belief will do is make it take longer to discover.

It's easy to follow a template. It's easy to do what's already been done.

But was that what you were brought on this earth to do? Was it to play someone else's game or to follow in someone else's footsteps?

I don't think so.

When you ride waves, you're always behind. You're always trying to catch up with the latest trend, the newest marketing tactic. Today it's Pinterest, yesterday it was Google Plus.

The question remains, will you attempt to frantically ride these waves or will you create your own?

Doing what's already been done is inevitably a much safer path than pioneering your own. However, going this route will mean that you will always be trying to catch up. You're always *following*, you're never ahead.

When you go with the flow, you're wave-chasing; you're *always in reactive mode.* You're never thinking strategically, you're just reactively trying to incorporate the latest trend into your own life.

This type of wave-chasing is not only arduous, but it's a never ending game. There will inevitably be a new fad, a new flavor of the month. You'll have to hurry to employ it just a little quicker than everyone else before it becomes outdated.

Trends inevitability fall out of vogue before long. Like any bandwagon that people jump on, it loses its luster.

Even if you don't feel that you are the "passionate type", going through these keys and exercises, you will come to find, that you are probably much more passionate than you really think. You've probably just been told it's not practical to be passionate.

All right, let's get to the fun part. Here are the seven keys to finding your passion, and setting your life on fire.

1. Give yourself permission to be passionate.

You may not think that this step is important, but it is absolutely critical. For the longest time, I did not pursue doing what I loved for a living, because I didn't think that I *deserved* to be passionate about my work. I thought sure, *other people* can be passionate about what they do, but there's only so much room in the world for people doing what they love. "*Someone has to grind it out and do the tedious work,*" That thought is as backwards as it gets. Everyone has the right to be passionate about what they do for a living. Everyone deserves to wake up excited about their lives. That is your birthright.

I would go so far as to say that the only reason tedious work *exists* is that people agree to do it. We're coming to the technological level that if people didn't agree to do that tedious work, we would find a way to automate it, or eliminate it.

So the first key is to give yourself permission to be passionate about the work that you do. And besides, haven't you ever thought that you're in a much better position to help others when *you* actually *care* about the work you do?

A great exercise for examining your beliefs around this is to look at how you view others that are passionate about their work.

Take out a sheet of paper or open your text editor. Now write down all the beliefs you have about people that you think are incredibly passionate about their work. What positive beliefs do you have about them? What are the negative beliefs you have about them? Which of these beliefs are assumptions?

This picture you have is ultimately a picture of yourself. How you feel about others is a reflection of how you feel about yourself. If you want to be a person that resonates, accepts and deserves being passionate about your work, it's your job to modify this mental picture.

The more your identity is aligned with a person that feels good about being passionate, the easier it will be for you to find passion and fulfillment in the work you do.

2. Allow yourself to explore.

Most people think that they need to find their One True Passion. Anything else is just not worth it; it's all or nothing. But when you have an "all or nothing" mindset, you miss out on all the other opportunities for living passionately that are available to you.

Within fulfillment and enjoyment of your work there is a spectrum of possibility.

On one end of the spectrum is work that you completely despise and would rather die than carry out. On the other end is work that you absolutely love and are ridiculously excited every time you even *think* about doing it. Now, between those two polls lies a vast range of possibilities for doing work that bores, makes you feel indifferent, stimulates, challenges, excites and makes you come alive.

Move in the direction of the work that makes you come alive. When pursuing doing what you love for a living, you may first find an option of doing something you *like* doing, then that might lead you to something you *love* doing, then that might lead you to something that makes the hair on your arms stand on end.

The more accustomed you get to moving in the direction of work that makes you come alive, the better you'll be at filtering out all the stuff that doesn't excite you.

Realize that you might first need to grow accustomed to liking your work, before you start loving it. If you've spent a long time in with an attitude of dread toward work, this will be especially applicable for you.

3. Take a look at what you're already doing.

Often times, there are many opportunities for doing what we love right under our noses; we just haven't noticed it yet. Sometimes this is because we don't think we could actually make a living out of it. Or it might just be because it never occurred to us that we found it so fascinating, because it always seemed so natural.

Here are a few questions to get yourself started:

•• What do you often find yourself searching for on Google and researching for hours?

•• Does a certain topic turn you on just thinking about it?

•• What do you have an addiction to learning more about?

•• What do you find yourself talking about for hours to the point of losing track of time?

•• When you enter a bookstore, which section do you naturally gravitate toward?

4. Ask yourself powerful questions.

The truth is, most people have never even given themselves enough time to figure out what they are really passionate about. That kind of time is simply not a priority. Other things tend to take precedence, like laundry and dentist appointments and watching other people live out their dreams on reality shows and comparing cell phone features online.

Everything else seems to take the front seat when it comes to life, everything other than exploring what makes you really come alive.

If you're going to have any hope at figuring out what it is that really makes you tick, you'll need to spend some time actually thinking about it. If you can't make that a priority, close this book now. It's not worth finishing.

Still here? Awesome. I'm glad that you decided discovering your passion is a priority. Nothing else will have a greater impact on your enjoyment of life.

So here's what you need to do: Take out your journal and answer these questions:

•• What would I do even if I didn't get paid to do it?

•• What gifts do I have that I would like to make available to the world?

•• When is a time in my life that I have felt the most creative?

•• What is incredibly easy to me?

•• What would I do if I got paid to exist?

•• What are one or two examples of great work I've done in the past?

These questions will jump start your subconscious mind. The important point is that you answer each question without thinking too much about it. Just allow yourself to write whatever comes to your mind. Let a link form between your heart and your fingertips.

Don't censor yourself at this point. You can always remove the really ridiculous stuff later.

Now what do you see? What patterns are showing up in your answers?

5. You might have to create it.

Realize that you may have a passion for doing something that doesn't yet exist. Computer programmers have been creating software for people that didn't know they needed it, until they created it. You might have to create your own profession, or your own job, through a hybrid of different fields. Don't limit yourself to conventional, template-like work paths.

Also, look for opportunities where you can fill a gap, where a need is not being adequately met in a specific industry. *Jitterbug* did this with creating a simpler cell phone that seniors could easily use.

I did this with creating a website for people that are turned off by typical self-help material. If you look for it, there is always a gap that you can exploit.

6. Test it.

There are many ways you can get a taste of your potential career, before you delve into a four year degree or thousands of dollars on seminars and information products.

Here are a few possibilities for testing your passion:

•• Take an adult education class at your local community college on your potential interest. This is a really cheap, fairly quick way to figure out if you have enough passion in that particular area.

•• Buy a couple of books on the subject, and see how long you can read about it before you lose interest. If you're still hungry after the first few books, it's probably sustainable.

•• Find someone who's already doing what you want to do, and interview them.

•• Do a search on Google, find someone in that field, send them an email and ask if they would mind answering a few short questions. Most people are more than happy to do this, and actually find it very flattering.

Once you've got some experience, now is the time to really test it. Create a website with a simple service offering around your topic.

Do this for a few weeks or months; if you haven't lost interest, you know there's a possibility for long-term fulfillment, and it's not just a fleeting fancy.

7. Look for fulfillment and happiness not riches.

A lot of people waste a lot of time trying to find a career that will make them rich. But the problem with this is that being rich is such a vague concept.

Money may give you temporary enjoyment, but they really don't get down to the core of it. You can be "happy" without being *rich!*

Instead of asking "What can make me rich?" ask "What makes me feel fulfilled?"

Sometimes that may be choosing work where you won't be famous, rule the world, or become extremely rich. What matters, though, is that what you're doing aligns with your values. If you value fame more than contribution, maybe you'll be more fulfilled as a reality TV celebrity (just don't expect people to remember you for very long).

But if you value relationships, community, and making a positive impact, you will probably be fulfilled in a more meaningful pursuit.

Before you choose to undertake a new endeavor, think about whether it makes you really feel fulfilled or not. Is it just something you find cool and interesting, or does thinking about doing it make you feel like you'd be making a difference?

That's where true passion and charisma comes from... making a difference in the lives of others.

Now... make it happen.

After you've found out *what* your passion is, it's time to start living it. It's time to get dirty in the messy business of living your bliss.

Immerse yourself in passionate, deliberate action, instead of perpetual toe-dipping.

Now that you've discovered your passion, the only question is... *How can you set this world on fire with it?*

Take the next step...

Reclaim your dreams

If you want to create something truly great, if you want to be number one in the race, **you absolutely must play your own game.**

Don't try to be the next Steve Jobs. Be the next *you.* Explore the uncharted stretches of your own path — the one that's waiting to be released inside you. The one that's dark, expansive and blissfully terrifying (yes, bliss and fear can actually coexist).

Stop trying to chase waves. Stop listening to the experts. Stop reacting to the latest and greatest.

Start creating your own game. Tear everything down and build your own empire from the ground up; on your terms.

It will be, perhaps, the hardest work of your life. But it will also, by far, be the most rewarding

9

Enjoy Life!

I am convinced you want to live a happy life! If you really desire that for yourself, then it's important to learn to enjoy life. Some people may think they can only enjoy life when they have a lot of money or have a successful career. But that's not true. You can enjoy your life, where you are, with what you already have. You can enjoy your life *now*.

Life is not a dress rehearsal! This is the real thing and you have one shot at making the best of it! I don't know about you, but I have spent years "sort of happy". I am determined to enjoy life!

There is one key that has caused me to see life differently and redefine what I considered joy: ***Slowing Down!*** You will be surprised how much we miss in the midst of our hustle and bustle.

I thought I would share with you a few things that have surprisingly brought me joy over the past few years *(This was my New Year Reflection of 2009)*

Appreciate Beauty. Each day we come across beauty in a number of shapes and forms. It's a shame, then, that many people have become so accustomed to this beauty that it goes largely unappreciated. I suggest looking again at the people, plants, gadgets, and buildings (to name but a few examples) around you and taking a moment to appreciate what makes them so special.

Connect With Nature. Nature is an amazing healer for the stresses and strains of modern life. Eating lunch in the park or watching the sunset, are just a few simple ideas for how you can enjoy the outdoors on a daily basis.

Laugh. E. E. Cummings once said "the most wasted of all days is one without laughter." How very true. Never be too busy to laugh, or too serious to smile. Instead, surround yourself with fun people and don't get caught up in your own sense of importance.

Have Simple Pleasures. A good cup of coffee when I first wake up; time spent talking to my girls about the adventures of their lives; cooking a nice meal in the evening; these may not seem terribly exciting, but they are some of the simple pleasures I enjoy in life. If you slow down for just a moment and take the time to appreciate these ordinary events, life becomes instantly more enjoyable.

Here are few things a few ladies shared about their life's simple pleasures:

"The fact that God loves me past my mistakes. To know that he loves me so much that everything he owns belongs to me. Also, my best job in the world, being a mother, brings me extensive amount of Joy. I so love being a mom." **Stacey Virgo, Orlando, Florida**

"Music and dancing speaks life to me when I'm feeling down!" **Keairra Bolden, Washington, DC**

"The tranquility of living near the water that soothes anything!" **LaTracey Copeland, Ocean Springs, Mississippi**

"Going outside early Sunday morning does it for me. It's like the earth is still quiet. There's calmness in the atmosphere. I love it!" **Janelle Middleton, New Castle, Delaware**

"Reading motivational quotes and speeches from some of the world's most prolific orators and intellectuals." **Ad Faulkner, *Chicago, Illinois***

"I enjoy looking up at the sky and seeing how beautiful the clouds are or seeing beams of sunlight shine through a gap between the clouds. I can be in bumper-to-bumper traffic, look up, and be in my happy place." **Danita L. Brooks, Capitol Heights, Maryland**

"Taking a long walk in nature listening to nothing but the sounds of Gods' wonder - no other distraction from anything or anyone! That brings me sheer joy, and I can use that time to speak to God about all of what's going on in my life and gain some clarity from Him." **Tamara Coleman, Jackson, Mississippi**

"One of my most favorite yet simple pleasures is to walk into the house husband and child free to have time to recollect my thoughts of the day... Just simply having time to myself. Being a wife and a mom can sometimes be so overwhelming but worth it all in the end." ***Carrita Barnes*, Waldorf, Maryland**

"Sitting Indian style on my bed writing a passage in my journal, and then flipping thru old passage's that I wrote trying to see if I have grown!!" **Yolanda Eiland-Brown, Waldorf, Maryland**

"The process of cooking, especially a new recipe." ***Monique Richardson, Raleigh, North Carolina***

You see, it doesn't always take something big to make a BIG difference in your day. Great days make up a great life!

Connect With People. In so many ways, it is our relationships with people that give us the most happiness in life. Perhaps, then, the best way to enjoy your life more is not to spend so much time focusing on succeeding and working, but rather to build rewarding relationships with people.

Now, it is important to seek out positive people to interact with but it is equally just as important to avoid putting yourself needlessly into situations that drain you or are harmful to your attitude. That's easy to do when we're talking about, say, Pessimistic Peter in the accounting department. He's not an integral part of your life, and it's realistic to avoid his rants in the break room.

What's not realistic is to avoid, say, a sister (who might always think she's a victim), or a best friend (who has a tendency to dwell on how nasty her ex-husband is), or a mother-in-law (who constantly nitpicks), or even a spouse or significant other (who likes to point out everything that's going wrong in your lives).

Obviously, I think it would be irresponsible, unwise, and even cruel to cut these relationships out of your life without a second thought. You see, while I stand by the importance of surrounding yourself with positive people, I also think that it's always a good idea to put work into improving and strengthening your closest relationships. Think about it this way: Relationships are a two-way street; you can't write them off without doing your part to make them work!

Remember, life is all about people. And the stronger your relationships are with your friends and loved ones, the happier you will be.

Celebrate Your Successes. During a normal day, we are sure to have some minor successes. Perhaps you have successfully dealt with a difficult customer, made a sale, or received a nice compliment for your work. These aren't events worth throwing a party for, but why not take a moment to celebrate your success? Share the experience with someone else, reward yourself with a nice lunch, or just give yourself a mental pat on the back.

Far too often we subscribe to the ridiculous notion that if we aren't improving all the time that we aren't worthy, which I have come to discover is absolute **foolishness!** Our happiness doesn't come from simply reaching our goals but rather celebrating them.

Change will happen, one step at a time; you won't reach your goals within a matter of days. That's why it's important to celebrate each step of the way. It has been said that it takes 10 years to become an overnight success. Yet so many people continue to forget how important small steps really are. You may think that meditating for 15 minutes each day won't help you in the long run. You may think that going for that walk every evening won't help keep you fit. Yet the reality is small movement never fails to produce results in the end.

When you start small and see that you are capable of succeeding (you **ARE** capable) you then have a foundation to work with. With each goal you reach take a moment and reflect on what you've done. I literally get chills when I think back to where I was years ago. It's because I took small steps (and celebrated the milestones in the process) that I am here today…HAPPY and Fulfilled.

How do you celebrate? That's entirely up to you. For you, it may be taking a day off of work and spending the day with your kids. Or maybe after reaching that fitness goal of yours you finally take family vacation to the beach. Be creative. Do anything that makes you feel good, assuming it's legal of course. 😉

Just because you're taking small steps doesn't mean that those steps aren't worthy. Appreciate and celebrate every step you take no matter how small it may be.

There's a myth that many self- improvement readers seem to have fallen for lately, and that is you have to be at your best 100 percent of the time. This myth causes a great deal of pain for those who believe it, because it's literally an impossible level to sustain. The truth is you can't be at the top of your game all the time. In an ideal world perhaps, but realistically speaking it's out of the question.

I'm all about hard work, but even the hardest of workers know when it's time to take time off to just have fun. Yet it's important not to confuse celebrate with stagnate. When you celebrate you're rejuvenating yourself. When you stagnate you're simply asking to be left behind.

Nonetheless, the self-improvement path shouldn't own your life.

It's OK to take a break and just be human. It's OK to celebrate your accomplishments. It's OK to mess up and not beat yourself up over it. Periodically, I take a day or two to just let loose. I'll go out with friends or stay up late doing nothing productive. During that time, I throw all the self-improvement ideas out the door and just am the non-superwoman that I am. You can do the same.

Hard work without celebration is a burn out waiting to happen. There has to be balance. If you're taking action just so you can use your cool red pen to cross off an item on your to do-list, you're producing nothing of value. You should be proud enough of your goals that you have no problem celebrating when you reach them. Again, don't confuse celebrating with being cocky or arrogant because there is a difference.

Drop the "self- improvement" mindset and just bask in your current level of personal growth. You can't grow without rest, everyone needs a break. When you celebrate your successes you feel good about yourself, and as a result it's likely you will continue to make a difference.

While I believe it's important to celebrate your success, I also believe it's important to celebrate your failures. Next time you fail try this: Celebrate your failure. Be grateful for the opportunity to learn. Be thankful for the reminder that you're not perfect. Value your relationship with failure for it will one day introduce you to success.

Nobody enjoys failing, but those who embrace it tend to be more successful. What is failure anyway? Another way to say lesson learned? Over the past few years I failed miserably at several things, but I've also had major successes. On the success side, I've started an awesome speaking and online professional development business; I've authored 3 books, shared my message with thousands of people, rebuilt a successful real estate business and have become a genuinely happier person.

However the path hasn't always been smooth. Over the past few years I've also lost friends (well, I know where they are, I just choose to leave them there!), battled with depression, and struggled with the ins and outs of business. I've bought products that ended up being worthless, I've wasted time networking with the wrong people, and said a bunch of regrettable things. Yet, when I look back at my failures I know that they were invaluable in bringing me to where I am today.

The truth is, right now you're exactly where you need to be and so am I!

The paradox of the self- improvement obsession is that it often makes us feel worthless instead of raising us up. The purpose of self-improvement isn't for you to become addicted to the constant need to improve. Self-improvement must be a choice not a reflex.

Stop looking at happiness as a final destination. Happiness doesn't lie in a destination but rather lies in the transportation of your life journey. Do you walk down your life path with open eyes and heart? Do you celebrate your success? Or do you remain a servant to the never ending path of improvement? Do your goals inspire you? Or are they just a means to an end?

Happiness isn't a stop. Improvement isn't a goal. Your inspiration comes from the fact that you are alive and enjoying life!

Disregard those silly people that say you're unworthy. Congratulate yourself on all you've done. ***You are enough.***

10

Stay Committed to Your Own Happiness

Who deserves your commitment to be happy?

Well an obvious first answer is that you do … although if you're like most people, your ego, your conditioned self, doesn't really agree and is doing everything possible to prevent your happiness. More on that momentarily…

But there are others who deserve your commitment to your happiness.

If you're a parent, your children most definitely deserve it. Aside from the basic necessities, in fact, there is arguably nothing they need and deserve *more* from you than you striving for your happiness.

The closer your spirit is to being fulfilled, the more you are able to *be there* for your kids, and the more you are able to guide them down the path to their own happiness.

Who doesn't know of, at least, a few mothers and fathers who run themselves ragged, who drive themselves close to a nervous breakdown, trying to please the kids, provide for the kids, give the kids "an edge," "prepare them for life"?

The drained and frazzled parents these kids are getting, and the lessons these kids are *really* learning from these drained and frazzled parents, work far, far harder *against* the children's own happiness than any benefit they are gaining.

And who doesn't know several divorced couples – and married couples – who fight, manipulate and emotionally drain one another in the name of being right and doing "what's right for the children" … all the while forgetting that what is most *wrong* for the children are parents who are fighting, manipulating and emotionally draining one another?

Remember, what you are most to your kids, even when you think they aren't watching, is an *example*.

This doesn't mean you can't make mistakes. You can, you will, and they can and will. It does mean that you should strive for peace and **being happy** -- and that, inasmuch as possible, you should try to help create an environment where your spouse, your ex (yes, your ex) and anyone who has an influence on your child's life can achieve their peace and happiness too.

If more than anything you want your children happy, then remember they are watching you – show them how to be happy by striving to *be* happy.

It's so Obvious that Everyone Seems to Forget It

Along similar lines, your parents deserve your commitment to being happy, too. Your mother, father, stepmother, stepfather, foster parents, grandparents or whoever you consider your true parents, wanted one thing above all else for you back when they were raising you – for you to be happy.

Whatever amount of time and effort they invested in raising you, and whether the job they did was mediocre or fantastic, what they most wanted – the same way you do or will for your children – is your happiness.

Dead or alive, no matter where they are, they still want this above all else for you now.

This does not mean your parents deserve you living according to what would make *them* happy – a common and dangerous misperception and the source of much angst between parents and even grown children. They deserve you living for and striving for what most makes *you* happy, even if it is not what they would choose.

It also seems obvious – but like so much that is obvious it is usually forgotten – that your spouse or significant other also deserves your commitment to happiness. They love you, so your happiness is extremely important to them.

Your happiness, or lack thereof, greatly impacts their own happiness. You want them happy; of course, because you love them. Therefore, you DO owe it to them to strive for your own happiness.

Put another way, for the skim readers, if you're not committed to being happy, how can anyone who loves you be fully happy?

In this sense, any siblings and other family who care about you and vice-versa, and all your true friends, deserve your commitment to your happiness. Your being happy makes them happier and you want them happy as they can be.

In still a larger sense, if you love the world, the universe, God, He deserves your commitment to your happiness, too. Your commitment to your joy breeds joy, and is your demonstration of your love and gratefulness for life.

For all these reasons, which all really amount to yourself – after all, yourself includes you but also your kids, your spouse or significant other, parents, extended family, friends, God, and the universe – you deserve your unflinching commitment to being happy.

But are You Letting Everyone Down If You're Not Being Happy?

You are not letting anyone down if you're currently not happy. While you and others deserve your *commitment* to happiness, everyone has to learn to accept that hardships happen, depression happens, the downsides of life happen, slipping out of happiness happens, and we're all human and won't always be happy.

But if you're currently not happy *and* you're not making it a priority to change that, then you *are* doing yourself – and therefore the others you care about – a major disservice. It is about the trying, about the striving, about the commitment to be happy.

In parallel, and by way of comparison, if you are unhealthy you are not letting anyone down … but you do owe it to yourself and those you care about to try to be healthier. You are wanted and needed here, after all.

Of course, just as it is not so simple as merely deciding to be healthier, your commitment to being happy is more than just a decision. The decision is an important start, but it is **action** that will get you there.

Fortunately, these 'actions' are enjoyable and so is this commitment to being happy! It is arguably THE key commitment of your life and possibly the most enjoyable! Life is good!

But there are two, all-too-common, barriers to happiness that you need to be aware of in order to bypass them. Would you like to know what or should I say WHO those barriers are? They are both **YOU!**

Barrier 1: "I Am WAY Too Busy To Do What Makes Me Happy!"

Imagine you are a sprinter in the Olympics. You stand at the starting line, waiting for the gun to go off to start the race … in your fluffy house slippers.

“Why are you wearing slippers?” the sprinter next to you whispers.

“Because I just didn’t have enough time today to put on my running shoes,” you respond.

It sounds ridiculous – your competition would surely think you’re joking or insane – and yet this is precisely the reasoning many people are trained to use when putting off or completely denying themselves the things that make them happy.

When you are stressed out, sad, angry, or otherwise encountering emotional barriers, do you embrace the experiences that provide you strength to effectively overcome the challenging emotions? Or do you abandon them?

Are you the type that thinks, “First I will work my issues out, and THEN I will do things I enjoy, things that fulfill me”? Do you insist on struggling first and then, only if you can squeeze it in somewhere, doing something you enjoy? If so, it is time to reprioritize your commitments.

In the same way a sprinter’s shoes are essential to helping her run a good race, your happiness is essential to helping you most effectively work through the challenges life presents you.

Happiness is not a reward. As much as food, water and sleep, happiness is the fuel itself. You need to make enjoying your life top priority if you wish to overcome life's challenges, if you wish to achieve your goals, and if you wish to achieve true success in all facets of your life.

If you find yourself not doing things that you personally enjoy every single day of your life; if you find yourself stuck in the mindset that you must struggle and merely survive before you can reward yourself with something you enjoy, then you are sabotaging your health, relationships, career, success, and your overall happiness. It is time to re-evaluate, reprioritize and make a real commitment to being happy.

Barrier 2: "Being Happy Makes Me Feel Guilty Anyway So the Heck with It"

For a variety of reasons I won't delve into here – media, religion, upbringing and/or other factors depending on who you are – ***most*** **people live with the script that the things they enjoy and desire are** ***bad*****.**

Indeed, there is a pervasive belief that pursuing your happiness and being happy means you are being selfish.

Happiness therefore makes people feel guilty. And people therefore shun what will make them happy.

Perverse when you think about it, isn't it?

But think about yourself: when you consider taking the time to do something you enjoy – even if in theory you know it is as important to your being as food and water -- does guilt surface inside you? Do you think you should be doing something "productive" *instead* of something you will enjoy? Getting bills done instead of getting a massage, for example? And if you actually DO the thing you enjoy, does even greater guilt surface inside you?

Perverse indeed…But mighty prevalent.

What you really need to remember to help you reprioritize is to trust your "pure self," not your "conditioned self" (a.k.a. ego.) The pure self is also known as the "creative self," "real self," and "free self" in different schools of psychology, but they all essentially mean the higher YOU who has not been manipulated and conditioned by the various social forces who don't necessarily have your personal best interests in mind. In short, go to your intuition and trust it.

What does your intuition tell you about happiness right now, for starters? Does it tell you that you should avoid pursuing the things that make you happy because it will offend others, make them see you as "high and mighty," a slacker, and all the rest?

Or does your intuition tell you that, indeed, your commitment to being happy is as essential to you as food, water and sleep (if not more so)?

What have you done today to enjoy your day?

What have you done to fulfill you?

You owe it to yourself … which of course means all those you love who comprise yourself, as well as yourself.

11

The Conclusion in a Nutshell

So Girl…what are you going to do with all that we have discussed? I have a suggestion:

Be Happy and Live a Drama Free Life!

No Matter How Big Your Situation, Stand Your Ground:

I've learned to live a fairly "drama free" life. It wasn't easy to do, but it's 100% possible! There are just a few things you have to accept:

First: You have to accept that you can't fix everything! There are going to be situations in your life that you can do absolutely nothing about! So, you can do one of two things; you can cry over it and throw yourself into a headache inducing pity party, or you can stand strong, take action and respond positively. Your response is your responsibility.

Second: Worry gets you nowhere! It doesn't solve your issues nor does it get you any closer to a solution! So, drop the worry!

Third: Cut some ties! If there are people in your life that are constantly contributing to your drama, as hard as it may seem, cut them loose! They will be hurt and maybe even angry, but if they aren't lifting you up, then they're tearing you down! Give them one chance and one chance only and if they can't be an encouragement to you then cut'em loose!

Fourth: Learn not to give dag-on ☺! Sounds funny, doesn't it? Well, it's true! If someone gets in your face and calls you all kinds of names, then smile and say "thank you". If someone jumps up in your business and calls you every name in the book, first ask yourself, "Is what they're saying true?", then smile and say "thank you". Don't sweat the small stuff! If it's not going to change your life or future in any way, then it's not worth letting it get to you! Got it? Good!

Lastly: Keep your chin up! Maintain a positive outlook and see the good side of things! Use your situation as a chance to grow stronger, smarter and wiser! Don't allow people to contribute to your mood! YOU control your emotions! Not your ex, your parents, your friends, or family! ONLY YOU!

Now, you may be asking yourself, how I know all of this will work! Because I live it!

Ladies, it's like the title of this book says...."Girl…Get Yourself Together!" It's not the situation that affects your life, but how you walk through it! You can either face your life lying down and feeling sorry for yourself; constantly worrying, which will eventually affect your health, or you can take the bull by the horns, dig your heels in and throw that bison on his back!

Take Responsibility for Your Life

This is a very important principle. As an adult, you are solely responsible for all the choices in your life. So many people look to blame others or circumstances for the things that are not right in their lives. This attitude is self-delusional; pretty much every long term situation that happens to us in our adult lives, can be traced back to some decision or lack of decision made by us either at a conscious or subconscious level, sometime in the past. Once we stop denying, blaming and whining and accept that we had our part to play in the circumstances, then we are in a better position to move forward and to learn from our mistakes.

What people often forget is that it is most often by our mistakes that we learn; if we deny our mistakes or fail to take responsibility, we fail to learn and improve. It is often those who go out into life, make mistakes and try again that are the most interesting people. Every mistake, every catastrophe is a life experience, part of their life story. By getting out there, not being frightened of making mistakes, learning from each chapter of their lives, they grow in wisdom and as a person. We all want to avoid mistakes but when things go wrong you should embrace the moment as an opportunity to learn and do better next time.

We must also recognize that we are responsible for the way we respond to people, actions, and events in our lives. In fact, in my view, one of the key determinants to how we perform in life is not defined by what actually happens to us, but rather how we respond to the events life puts in our way. If your relationships with others if not going well, you need to examine your own behavior. It is often the case, that people you interact with will "mirror" your attitude at a subconscious level. So if you are angry or full of resentment, this may come across in your words or body language and you will receive an angry or resentful response. The reality is, if you had approached the situation in a positive and open frame of mind, the outcome would almost certainly have been considerably different, with a positive outcome.

You are responsible for your *NOW*. If you hold anger or resentment or hurt for people or events in the past, it is important to try to deal with this or you will never Get Yourself Together and experience that happy life that you deserve.

Remember we often blame people from the past or hold resentment, but the truth is, they may well have done the best they could, given the limitations of their knowledge, background, and awareness. Life is a rich tapestry and sometimes the threads that run through it contain hurt and pain. Remember nothing is finished until it is done, do not let those threads define your whole picture, rather let them highlight the threads of joy and love that you can choose to weave into your life. **You have a choice.**

It's time to make your life Drama Free! C'mon Girl…Get Yourself Together and Let's Do this Thing Called Life on TOP!

Letter from the Author

Hey Ladies:

When I embarked upon this project, which has required so many hours of my time, it was my heart to see you live life to its fullness! The book evolved into a movement!

Most of us are overworked, underappreciated, lost in our many "hat wearing" lives and we need to get ourselves together! We need to get away and be renewed and reminded that we are fully equipped and able to handle all that we are charged to handle. We need to get a grip!

It's amazing to me how many ladies lose themselves as the years go by and we need to get ourselves together and get moving with our dreams and visions! I started the Annual Girls Getaway Conference for this very reason.

Please make sure you visit me at www.robynspeaks.com and stay up to date with Conference Dates and Events in your area.

I am looking forward to meeting each one of you soon!

Believing in Your Success!

Robyn

About the Author

Robyn Y. Smith: *Author, Speaker, Entrepreneur*

Robyn has owned and operated over 10 successful businesses in her career. She is a successful entrepreneur and is currently the CEO of Success Builders Network/Seminars, a Professional Development Company; COO of The Visions Group, LLC, a Residential and Commercial Property Management Real Estate Firm; A Certified Distressed Property Expert and Founder of robynSPEAKS!, a Personal and Professional Motivational Company, providing authored books, motivational seminars, professional and personal coaching and the sponsor of SBN's Annual Girls Getaway Conference.

Robyn, along with her husband, started Visions Realty. In 2004 and quickly became one of Maryland's Top Brokers. By 2005 Visions Realty had over 100 agents with $100,000,000 in sales.

Becoming a motivational speaker, author and success coach had been her dream since she was just twenty one years old. It took her over two decades to make her dream a reality because she didn't think she was ready to speak in front of people. When asked why she waited so long to live out her dream, she says it was real simple. "I didn't think people would listen. I kept making excuses like I am too young or I am not successful enough. I didn't know what it meant to be successful. I thought if I had four cars and a giant home that I would be successful enough so that people would listen to me. I kept telling everyone that when I have ten real estate offices, I will become a motivational speaker."

Then came the event that changed it all. Robyn says the best thing that ever happened to her was the worst thing that happened to her...the mortgage and real estate market crash of 2008. Everything that she worked for, seemingly, was about to be lost. "It was a struggle to keep everything above water, but I used what I had learned from years of studying and sitting under mentors such as my Pastors and other great teachers such as Tony Robbins, Dale Carnegie, Napoleon Hill and others, and I regrouped and reposition myself and my business."

This life changing experience led to successes she never

imagined possible. (Well, actually, she really did!) Robyn decided to write books about her life changing experience so the average person could achieve greatness just like she was experiencing.

Her message will empower you to change the negatives of your life into the greatest positives by motivating you to pursuit your dreams and desires. Robyn has been sharing her compelling story with business leaders, college students, sales professionals and troubled teens, and anyone who has gone through difficult times.

Robyn's Commitment to You

Robyn's commitment is to help everyone achieve their business and personal goals, while making the world a better place one thought at a time. Robyn will help you gain control of your thoughts, allowing you to manifest the most desirable outcomes in your career and your relationships, while you live the life of your dreams. Robyn will help you overcome previous failures while you turn your negatives into the greatest positives of your life. Robyn will show you how she used, what could have been the lowest point of her business career, as her catalyst of change, getting her to live the life she only dreamed of.

Once you are a master of your thoughts and your feelings, you will feel compelled to help others achieve similar results that are now your everyday realities. When you help people grow with your wisdom, you are a part of a humanitarian effort that will make this world a better place for you and me and most importantly for the children of our future. Let's focus on our future while we become masters of our destinies!

Contact us

Success Builders Network &

robynSPEAKS

www.robynspeaks.com

1-888-617-6066

SUCCESS BUILDERS NETWORK

robynSPEAKS!

Notes

Notes

Notes

Notes